Old KILLIN, KENMORE and LO~~~~~

by
Bernard Byrom

A panoramic view over Loch Tay from the south west. The photograph must have been taken before 1897 because the Lyon Villas near the railway station (page 11) had not yet been built. The village of Killin lies to the centre and right of the photograph with the Killin Hotel and parish church prominent over to the left. Beyond the village the railway runs in a straight line across the photograph and the white-roofed station shelter can be seen at the end of the road curving away from the village. The River Lochay enters from the left and winds its way towards the point where it joins the loch. On its final bend it is joined from the right by the River Dochart which has already thundered its way over the Falls of Dochart at the approach to Killin, and flowed past the MacNab's ancient burial ground of Inch Buie and under the castellated viaduct near Kinnell House. On the left bank the promontories near Morenish can be seen jutting into the waters of the loch and, further along, the shoreline bends left towards the old village of Lawers which is out of sight in the photograph. On the right the promontory by Fiddlers Bay is the most noticeable feature before the shoreline curves inwards and obscures Ardeonaig from view. Finally, the loch sweeps further north-eastwards to Kenmore where it funnels to become the mighty River Tay, the longest of all Scotland's rivers.

ACKNOWLEDGEMENTS

The author wishes to thank: Breadalbane Folklore Centre, Killin; Norman Brett, Loch Tay Boating Centre, Kenmore; Donald Campbell, Kenmore; Frances Chassar, Kenmore Post Office and Factor for the Taymouth Castle Estate; Karen Cole, Taymouth Trading Company, Kenmore; Steve Connelly and Jan Marchant, Perthshire Archives, A.K. Bell Library, Perth; Jeremy Duncan, Local History Librarian, A.K. Bell Library, Perth; Peter & Sara Gottgens, Ardeonaig Hotel; Rev. Kenneth MacVicar, Kenmore; Elizabeth McDiarmid, Lawers; John and Helen Taylor, Ardeonaig.

FURTHER READING

The books listed below were used by the author during his research. None of them are available from Stenlake Publishing. Those interested in finding out more are advised to contact their local bookshop or reference library.
The Statistical Accounts of Scotland, 1791–99 and 1845.
Survey of Tayside, 1769.
Jeremy Duncan, *Perth and Kinross: The Big County*, 1997.
Duncan Fraser, *Highland Perthshire*, 1978.
Duncan Fraser, *400 Years Around Kenmore*.
C.E.J. Fryer, *The Callander & Oban Railway*.
W.A. Gillies, *In Famed Breadalbane*, 1938.
Seton Gordon, *Highways and Byways in the Central Highlands*, 1935, republished 1995.
Nick Haynes, *Perth and Kinross: An Illustrated Architectural Guide*, 2000.
Brid Hetherington, *Under the Shadows*.
Archie McKerracher, *Perthshire in History and Legend*, 1998, revised 2000.
Joan Pearson, *Tales of the Tay*, 2003.
John Thomas, *The Callander & Oban Railway*, 1966, updated by J. Farrington 1990.

An Edwardian family picnic on the northern shores of Loch Tay, about a mile west of Kenmore. This spot is only easily accessible by boat and the rolled-up trouser legs of the man on the right suggest that he is the boatman who has been hired to row the picnickers to the bay. It is apparent from the position of the boat that he had to jump into the water and haul it far enough up onto the shore for his genteel passengers to climb out without getting their feet wet.

INTRODUCTION

It is impossible to write any account of Loch Tayside without referring to the enormous influence the Campbells of Breadalbane had on the history of the area.

The area called Breadalbane – which means the heights of Alban – cannot be precisely defined but can roughly be said to extend from the east end of Loch Tay at Kenmore to the western end of Strathfillan at Tyndrum. It therefore encompasses all the scenes in this book.

How did the Campbells acquire their power and influence in this area? They gained their properties by a mixture of strategic marriages, aggression and dubious legal manoeuvres. By these means they were able to acquire such an area of land that, by the end of the nineteenth century, the whole of the countryside from Kenmore to Oban belonged to them. At the height of their power their estate extended to 437,696 acres and was over 100 miles long. From relatively humble beginnings in the fifteenth century the third Marquis of Breadalbane was, by the time of the First World War, the largest landowner in Britain.

A satirical poem published in *Punch* in February 1903 began thus:

> From Kenmore
> To Ben More
> The land is a' the Marquiss's
> The mossy howes,
> The hethery knows,
> An' ilka bonnie park is his.

Much of the property they owned had been seized from the outlawed Clan MacGregor by 'Grey' Colin Campbell who became the sixth Laird in 1650. He was succeeded by his son, known as Black Duncan of the Cowl, who outdid even his father in greed and ruthlessness. He erected several castles to protect his territories and hunted down and executed anyone who dared stand in the way of his acquisitive ambitions. The Campbells' policy at this time, as written in the 'Black Book of Taymouth' was 'Conquess and keepit things conquessit.'

Black Duncan died in 1631 and fourteen years later his enemies had their revenge when the Campbells' arch-enemy, the Marquis of Montrose (a prominent member of the Graham clan) swept through the countryside in support of King Charles I. He laid waste to the whole of Breadalbane and, as a result, the estate became heavily burdened with debt.

The situation was rectified by Duncan's great-grandson John Campbell who in 1657, at the age of 22, married the appropriately named Lady Mary Rich, daughter of the Earl of Holland. They returned to his castle at Balloch with two ponies, he and his bride riding on one whilst the second carried her dowry of £10,000 in gold and was guarded by two heavily-armed Highlanders running alongside. A huge fortune indeed in those days!

In 1676 John was created first Earl of Brea d'Albyne and Holland and the family once again began to prosper. With the country now more settled the second and third Earls of Breadalbane began to improve their estates, introducing flax growing and establishing lint mills and spinning schools. The district was well populated and it was reported in 1769 that there were 1,786 persons living on the north side of Loch Tay and about 1,200 on the south side. The third Earl set up spinning schools in various parts of the district and gave away a number of spinning wheels each year. In 1770 alone the amount of flax dressed at Lawers was 460 stones (2,925 kilos) and at Killin 954 stones (6,060 kilos). The yarn was bought by merchants who sold it on at markets in cities such as Perth and Glasgow where it was manufactured into cloth.

It was the third Earl who laid out the present village of Kenmore in 1760 as well as building the main road from Kenmore to Killin along the north side of Loch Tay, whilst the fourth Earl introduced more modern farming methods. By the time the first *Statistical Account of Scotland* was compiled in 1793 the population of Kenmore and Killin parishes numbered over 5,000 souls and it was reckoned that there were around 4,000 cattle and 42,000 sheep on the hillsides.

The fourth Earl demolished the family's castle at Balloch in 1799 and in its place built a magnificent new edifice which he named Taymouth Castle. He was created first Marquis of Breadalbane in 1831 and died in 1834.

His son succeeded him as the second Marquis and is most remembered for following the popular fashion of evicting his tenants and replacing them with sheep. By 1840 over 500 families had been evicted from their tenancies, many of them emigrating to the New World. However, these evictions and the lure of better-paid work in the Lowland factories were the start of the depopulation of the area. In fairness to the Marquis, the scale of his evictions was nothing like as great as some of his Highland neighbours, notably the Duke of Sutherland.

The spectacular entertainment of the 23-year-old Queen Victoria and Prince Albert at Taymouth in 1842 was surely the high point of the family's history. In her journal the Queen wrote, 'It seemed as if a great chieftain in olden feudal times was receiving his sovereign. It was princely and romantic.' In the evening the grounds were illuminated; there were fireworks and bonfires on the hillside whilst Highlanders danced by torchlight in front of the house. The young Queen wrote ecstatically, 'I never saw anything so fairy-like'.

The second Marquis died childless in 1862 and, after lengthy litigation, Gavin Campbell was declared third Marquis in 1885. The First World War brought greatly increased taxation and its aftermath brought economic depression locally. Some land was sold in 1920 but mounting expenses and death duties led to the Breadalbane Estates being broken up on the death of the third Marquis in 1922.

The castle and surrounding 400 acres were sold for £44,000 (pre-war valuation, £377,000). The contents fetched £24,000 over a six-day sale, the seventeenth century state coach being sold for a mere £11. Many of the purchasers were sporting tenants or local farmers and Taymouth itself was purchased by a business syndicate who formed The Taymouth Castle Hotel Company Ltd. Prior to the Second World War, they operated the castle as a luxury hotel and turned the deer park into a golf course.

Further sales followed and by 1948 nothing was left of their estates. Over nearly 500 years the Campbells of Glenorchy had put together the greatest landowning ever seen in Britain, but it took a mere 28 years for it all to be dissipated.

But their legacy can be seen everywhere in the area covered by this book. Whether the reader is interested in churches, hostelries, steamships, railways, local industry or simply houses, there is a strong likelihood that the object of their interest was provided or partially funded by one of the Campbells of Breadalbane. And even if they were often ruthless towards their enemies, at least they had a generally benevolent influence on their estates and on the lives of their tenants.

Happy browsing!

In 1883 the people of Killin, led by the Marquis of Breadalbane, financed the building of a railway from the steamer pier on Loch Tay to a junction with the Callander & Oban Railway, 5½ miles further west at a new station named Killin Junction. The latter was purely an interchange station for passengers between the main line from Glasgow to Oban and the branch to Killin and Loch Tay, and had no road access. There was one intermediate station, located on the outskirts of Killin village, about a mile short of the pier. After many financial setbacks, which included replacing the original contractor who had seriously underestimated the cost of the project, the line eventually opened to passenger traffic in March 1886. Although it was operated from the outset by the Caledonian Railway Company, the Killin Railway remained nominally independent until 1923 when it became part of the London, Midland & Scottish Railway Company. The line going out of the left of the picture ran into the single-platformed Loch Tay Station, from where passengers walked onto the pier to board the steamers. These sailed the length of Loch Tay to Kenmore, from where a stagecoach could take them the few miles to Aberfeldy and a railway connection to the Highland Railway's Perth–Inverness line at Ballinluig. The one-mile section of line between Loch Tay Pier and Killin was closed to passengers on 1 September 1939 and to goods traffic in November 1964. The remaining section between Killin and Killin Junction was closed on 28 September 1965 following a serious landslide in Glen Ogle which caused the closure of the whole of the Callander & Oban line between Dunblane and Crianlarich; ever since through trains from Glasgow to Oban have been routed via the West Highland line. At the time of writing plans are afoot to reopen the line between the village and the pier.

The mill on the Dochart at Killin was originally a meal mill and is thought to have been founded by St Fillan himself (in the early years of the eighth century AD he converted many of the local inhabitants to Christianity). It stands upstream of the old road bridge and adjacent to the spectacular Falls of Dochart. The present building dates from 1840 and Finlay McDiarmid is recorded as being the miller in 1889. Eight years later his widow is recorded as running the mill. It was owned by the Wilson family from 1912 and it subsequently became a woollen mill. Tweeds were woven here until 1939 and a lade, which still runs past the mill, carried water from here to another tweed mill in the village. In 1988, after several years of disuse, the building was bought by Stirling District Council and the people of Killin who raised money through public subscription. After two years of refurbishment, which cost £500,000, the mill was reopened in July 1994 as the Breadalbane Folklore Centre. The old mill wheel still stands at the side of the building but is no longer turned by the lade which is now disused. St Fillan's healing stones, which he is said to have left in the care of the miller, are still housed in the mill and each year they are embedded in fresh straw according to ancient custom. The old mill house stands to the left of the mill. It is nowadays a private house named 'Millmore'. The style of the windows has changed and the attics are no more, but otherwise the building is still recognisable.

The ancestral burial ground of the MacNabs is on the small isle of Inch Buie which is set in the River Dochart just downstream of the old road bridge at Killin. The name is derived from the Gaelic 'Inch Buidh' which means 'Yellow Island' because of its golden-coloured turf. At the eastern end of the isle is a stone enclosure in which are buried fifteen high-ranking members of the clan including nine chiefs; other members are buried outside its walls. The Clan MacNab's historical territory stretched from the western end of Loch Tay and Killin through Glen Dochart to Tyndrum. Their chiefs were traditionally descended from the younger son of Kenneth McAlpine who was Abbot of Glen Dochart and Strathearn; in Gaelic their name is 'Mac an Aba' meaning 'Son of the Abbot'. The setting is certainly wonderful. Indeed, one chief of the clan made an unsuccessful proposal of marriage to a young lady with the enticement that he owned the most beautiful burial ground in Scotland! The round stone ornaments have disappeared from the corners of the enclosure but the carved heads in the middle of the walls still look down benignly on the sleeping residents and visitors.

The Bridge of Lochay Hotel at Killin was built in 1765. It was originally a coaching inn beside the bridge over the River Lochay; the road over the bridge runs to the right of the picture. A stone outside the hotel entrance bears the inscription 'CHW 1765'. The location is on the western end of Loch Tay, a short distance east of Killin, and the small white building behind the trees is the old Toll Cottage (it still bears that name). Its occupant at the time of the 1891 census was James Craig, road contractor, along with his wife and their seven young children. The bridge itself was originally built in 1627 by Sir Colin Campbell. In the 1920s and '30s the proprietor of the hotel was James Hood who also hired out motor cars to visitors. The sign on the left of the picture appears to be advertising his garage services. In 1935 the hotel was used as a setting in the shooting of Alfred Hitchcock's film, *The Thirty-Nine Steps*. Nowadays the porch has been extended to the left to enlarge a lounge and to the right to make a small office; otherwise the aspect is virtually unchanged.

After the MacNab's castle at Eilean Ran in Glen Lochay was burned down by the combined forces of the Campbells and Oliver Cromwell's men in 1654, they made Kinnell House at Killin their principal seat. Its most legendary resident was Francis MacNab, who was born there in 1734 and succeeded his father as chief in 1788. He was very much a ladies man and, although he never married, was reputed to be the father of scores of children. On one occasion he appeared in a court case brought against him by a lady and her counsel referred to him as being the father of a hundred children. Francis was outraged at this accusation: 'Ye lying deevil!' he shouted, 'Ninety, maybe, but no' a hoondred!' During Francis's lifetime a porridge cart used to set out every morning from Kinnell House and call at several houses in the village, dispensing breakfast for his bairns! Over the centuries the power of the MacNabs waned and was supplanted by the power of the Campbells of Breadalbane. But by the twentieth century the position had been reversed and the MacNabs were able to re-purchase Kinnell House when the Breadalbane estates were sold off in the 1920s. In 1959 a new chief was recognised and he lived at Kinnell until his death in 1970, but today the house is no longer occupied by the MacNabs.

The hotel stands on the banks of the River Lochay and occupies the site of the old Streethouse Inn which was a refreshment stop for the Aberfeldy to Tyndrum coach in the seventeenth century. Extensive additions were made to the building in 1845, by which time it was known as the Commercial Hotel. By 1872 the hotel was advertising that a four-horse coach ran to and from the station in connection with all the trains and that its 'Posting and Hiring Establishment' was now complete. The station in question was the temporary terminus of the Callander & Oban Railway four miles distant at Glenoglehead; the line was not extended to Tyndrum until 1873 and did not reach Oban until 1880. In the meantime the hotel was served by a coach which ran from Aberfeldy via Kenmore to Killin and another on the same route which continued via Inverarnan to Fort William. A disastrous fire broke out on the night of 20 December 1941, starting in the upper part of the hotel and completely gutting the main part of the building. The alarm was raised by the Tayside Observer Corps which saw flames shooting through the roof. The local part-time firemen tackled the blaze until they were joined by the main brigade from Perth and a unit from Crieff. All the guests escaped unharmed. To the right is the corner of the parish church, built in 1744 and rebuilt in 1832 with seating for 905.

Little could these elegant ladies, relaxing in their wicker chairs in the lounge of the Killin Hotel in 1935, imagine that in only another six years the hotel would be gutted by a major fire and the area in which they were sitting would be reduced to rubble. Constructed entirely of glass and wood, the lounge was built onto the front of the hotel and extended from the entrance porch to the end of the building. When the hotel was rebuilt after the fire, the frontage was completely remodelled. The lounge walls were constructed of stone and it gained a curved perspex roof, whilst the previous six front bedrooms were increased to eight.

This impressive five-arch viaduct over the River Dochart at Killin was the most substantial structure on the railway branch line from Killin Junction to Loch Tay. It was built between 1883 and 1885. Because of the sometimes violent behaviour of the river it was constructed in the new material of concrete and the cost of its building was one of the reasons for the railway's original contractor running into financial difficulties. This picture shows the view of the viaduct from the isle of Inch Buie, looking towards Killin with the mighty Ben Lawers towering in the background. The railway closed in 1965 but the viaduct, with its ornate battlements in keeping with the nearly Kinnell House, survives as part of a public footpath and cycleway along the trackbed from the village through to the site of the steamer pier.

In 1897 a local man, Duncan Campbell, built a select development of six villas on the eastern outskirts of Killin. He named them 'Lyon Villas' and numbered them 1–6. Two years later he added a further five villas numbered 7–11. He himself is recorded as occupying Nos. 8 and 9. The estate was completed by the construction of Dreadnought Place which was owned by Alex MacNab, a farm manager, and comprised two houses with shops and five other houses. The estate was conveniently situated for Killin Station which can be seen in the middle distance to the right of the houses. The line was on a steeply falling gradient of 1 in 50 all the way from the main line at Killin Junction to Killin Station where it levelled out for the rest of the way to Loch Tay Pier. The sudden change in gradient can be clearly seen in the photograph where the line reaches the station. The villas are still there but are now surrounded by a larger housing development; the small hayricks in the field have been replaced by an estate of more modern houses, whilst the trackbed has become a pathway. The single-platform station with its wood-and-brick shelter is no more and the site of the station yard is occupied by a council depot, a roads maintenance depot and a car park.

The single-platformed station at Killin was located on the eastern outskirts of the town. The line's terminus was a mile further down the track at Loch Tay Station which served the steamer pier for boats to Kenmore. In the other direction the line joined the Callander & Oban Railway at Killin Junction, from where passengers could catch direct trains to Oban, Callander, Stirling, Glasgow and Edinburgh. The line was opened in 1886, but lost its passenger services between Killin and Loch Tay Station on the outbreak of war in 1939 (although freight services continued until 1964). The remaining service to Killin Junction was closed to all traffic on 28 September 1965. This 1950 photograph of the station shows a smart appearance and the track is laid on modern concrete sleepers. Although the railways were nationalised on 1 January 1948 as 'British Railways', the billboards still bear the initials (LMS) of the previous owners, the London, Midland & Scottish Railway Company.

A tranquil scene at the east end of Killin's Main Street. The road from Kenmore enters from the right and is joined on the left by the road leading from the station yard. The name above the shop on the right appears to be 'Moss, Stationers' and a poster in its window is prominently advertising F. & J. Smith's 'Glasgow Mixture' cigarettes. A man stands outside with a pair of tall stepladders and a bucket. Is he a billposter or just a window cleaner? The shop on the extreme right of the picture sells refreshments and the sign in its window advertises Cadbury's cocoa and chocolate. The cart heading towards the village centre has come from the direction of the station yard and looks to be loaded with sacks of provisions for delivery in the village. On the left a group of well-dressed Edwardian ladies standing outside what is nowadays the Craigbuie Guest House look on whilst a shepherd and his dog, attended by a group of inquisitive children, drive a flock of sheep towards the station yard.

This photo is the opposite view to the previous, although it was probably taken a few years later. The buildings on the left of the picture are still standing. The building on the far left is now the Shutters' Restaurant & Coffee Shop, followed by what are now Corrie Crafts, Killin Gallery & Antiques, the Co-operative shop and an Outdoor Centre. The buildings on the right have fared less well. The nearest thatched house, Rose Cottage, is still there, but the old cottages beyond it have been demolished and replaced by new buildings housing the police office, the post office and, set back from the road, the fire station. The stone buildings further down the road have survived. The nearest building is now the Craigbuie Guest House and the bow-fronted one beyond it, named Loch Tay Cottage, is still a private house. The building at the end of the street, where the road to Kenmore bears off to the left and the road to the station bears to the right, is St Fillans Episcopal Church. It was built of corrugated iron by the seventh Earl of Breadalbane in 1876 as a private chapel and was, for many years, open only in July and August, being staffed by prominent English clergymen on holiday in the area. It was closed in 1939 on the outbreak of the Second World War, but reopened in 1948 for full-time worship.

This view of the west end of Main Street is almost unchanged today apart from the loss of the old thatched cottage on the right of the picture. This photograph was taken around 1904 when most houses in the village didn't have a mains water supply. The lady on the right is drawing water from a cast-iron standpipe. However, by that time the village did appear to have a certain amount of street lighting – note the gas lamp standing between the houses on the right. The main road to the left leads shortly to the old mill (now the Breadalbane Folklore Centre) and onto the old bridge over the river by the Falls of Dochart. The road to the right is the minor road which runs along the north side of the River Dochart and eventually joins the A85 Crianlarich road near Auchlyne. The building in the centre is the forge owned for many years by the McFarlane family. They lived in the adjoining house which they named 'Riverview'. Alexander McFarlane is listed as the owner in 1888 and his descendants were still blacksmiths many years later. The smithy closed in the late 1960s or early '70s and the building is no longer in industrial use, whilst the house is now the Riverview bed & breakfast establishment.

Nothing now remains of these old thatched houses which once lined Gray Street, forming the approach to Killin from the west. The scene looks nineteenth century but the photograph was actually taken in the late 1920s and the cottages survived until late into the twentieth century. The River Dochart flows on the other side of the left-hand wall whilst, in the distance, the road dips and bends left to cross the river by the Falls of Dochart. Victorian census records and valuation rolls show the inhabitants to have been mainly local tradesmen. Once upon a time St Fillan's Quigrich was kept in one of these cottages. This was the head of his crozier which, around the time of the ninth century, was encased in bronze and covered with ornate panels of silver filigree. Sometime around the fourteenth century a silver-gilt case was made to house this relic and the silver filigree was transferred from the head of the crozier onto the sides of this case. After many adventures over the centuries both are now housed in the Scottish National Museum of Antiquities. The cottages have all been replaced by modern bungalows which have been built in a similar style to the originals, giving them an appearance in sympathy with the old cottages that are still standing further along the road to the village.

In 1873 the Earl of Breadalbane converted 'a nice little cottage' about one mile east of Killin into the more stately Auchmore House. However, this was only one of his many residences in the area and he does not appear to have spent much time living here. The 1891 census lists the house as having 59 rooms with windows (a sign of wealth) and the only occupants at that time as being the housekeeper and her mother! Earlier, its most celebrated visitors had been Queen Victoria and Prince Albert, who were rowed from Kenmore to Auchmore at the end of their visit to Taymouth Castle in September 1842. The royal barge was specially constructed for the occasion and was manned by eight oarsmen and accompanied by four other barges conveying the Earl of Breadalbane and his guests. During the Second World War, after most of Breadalbane estates had been sold, the house was used as a hospital for Polish soldiers. It survived until the early 1960s, but when it was discovered that it was suffering from extensive dry rot it was unceremoniously blown up. Only parts of the original complex of buildings, pictured above, survive as part of the present-day Auchmore House, a much smaller-scale affair that was built in the 1960s.

The Breadalbane mausoleum was founded in 1523 by Sir Colin Campbell, an ancestor of the Earls of Breadalbane, who built it close to the east side of the Campbell's stronghold of Finlarig Castle near Killin. According to the 'Black Book of Taymouth', it was intended to be 'ane burial place for himself and his posteritie' In 1829 it was rebuilt as a Tudor-style chapel, constructed in brick with a cement rendering that made it appear to have been built of stone. Fourteen chiefs of the clan lie within its walls. Although this photograph shows the mausoleum in all its glory, it had already become a crumbling ruin by the time that the last of the Campbells of Glenorchy died in the early years of the twentieth century. Buried outside its walls at their own request, and their graves marked with Celtic crosses, are Sir Gavin Campbell, third Marquis of Breadalbane (died 1922) and his wife of 50 years, Lady Alma St Fillan (died 1932) – the last of the Breadalbanes. Today the mausoleum presents a sorry sight. Its broken walls rise no higher than the top of the porch and the chapel has been filled with rubble, making it impossible to view the interior. Notices have been posted warning the visitor of the extreme danger of entering the mausoleum or the adjacent castle ruins.

Two stately ladies on view at Kenmore Pier. The sky may be overcast but the waters of the loch are placid and reflective as the *Lady of the Lake* leaves Kenmore Pier with a good complement of passengers, whilst the *Queen of the Lake* awaits her turn of duty. On the end of the pier a group of onlookers wave to the passengers on the departing ship, most of them no doubt wishing that they too could be on board. The service from Kenmore zigzagged across the loch from point to point. It generally called at Acharn, Fearnan, Lawers, Ardtalnaig and Ardeonaig, before reaching Killin less than three hours later. There, at Loch Tay Pier, a train to Killin Junction would connect with the steamer for the benefit of passengers heading for the main line westbound to Oban and the western Highlands or southbound down Glen Ogle to Callander, Stirling and the south. The regular steamer service was maintained until the outbreak of the Second World War in 1939, when it was withdrawn as an economy measure. It was never reinstated after the end of the war; all the steamer piers were demolished or left to rot, and the two ships never sailed again. The pier area at Kenmore is now occupied by the Loch Tay Boating Centre. At the time of writing a steamship is in the course of being built by a new company, the Loch Tay Steam Packet Company, which will replicate the decor and atmosphere of the old steamers on the loch and will once again sail from Kenmore.

A group of Edwardian children enjoying the summer sunshine, lined up for the photographer on the foreshore at Kenmore. In days gone by this area was used by the women of the village as a drying area for clothes. An unexplained phenomenon occurred here in 1794 when, without warning, the waters of the loch inexplicably receded as far west as Spray Island. The gabled building in the background is the United Free Church which was built by the second Marquis of Breadalbane in 1844. A year earlier a major schism which came to be known as the 'Disruption' had occurred in the Church of Scotland when a significant number of its members broke away from the established church and formed themselves into the Free Church of Scotland. In Kenmore, under the Marquis's influence, a large portion of the parish church congregation joined the Free Church and he built this church for their worship. Nothing much has changed in this view apart from the church building now being the premises of the Taymouth Trading Company and there is a car park behind where the children are standing.

The approach to Kenmore from Aberfeldy and the south loch road, around 1910. Road traffic was light in those days so the car driver and his passengers would not have worried about driving on the wrong side of the road! The Free Church building is on the left of the photo, with two artisan's cottages beyond it on the slope leading up to the village centre. The row of houses beyond them form the southern portion of the village square. At the top of the road is the village's hotel which has undergone a number of name changes over the years. At that time it was called the Breadalbane Hotel but by the 1920s its name had changed to the Kenmore Hotel. The Free Church closed as a place of worship many years ago and is now occupied by The Taymouth Trading Company Gift Shop and Tea & Coffee Room. The cottage nearest to it was demolished to make way for a police station, but this itself has closed and is now a private house whilst the adjoining cottage is now derelict.

Two charabancs are lined up in the Square outside the hotel whilst, near the main door, a well-dressed lady appears to be boarding her private carriage driven by a top-hatted groom. In the background a delivery cart is on its rounds of the cottages. The low-roofed building next to the hotel was the old school. This closed in 1873 and later became the Masonic Hall. It is now part of the hotel. The original village was called Inchadney and was located about two miles away (on the opposite bank of the Tay) on a ford crossing of the River Tay. The whole village was moved lock, stock and barrel to its new location in 1540 when Balloch Castle was built. The present-day Kenmore was created as a model village by the third Earl of Breadalbane who built cottages on either side of the Square in 1760 and a bridge over the Tay in 1774. The village was laid out on a T-Plan to the east of Kenmore Church. The houses were initially single storey but in the mid-nineteenth century they were raised half a storey and given rustic porches and dormers. The cottages were provided for local people free of charge as long as they brought a skill to the area. The villagers lived rent-free on condition that they kept their homes clean and in good repair. At the time of the 1795 *Statistical Account* the principal occupations in the parish were those of weavers, tailors, wrights, shoemakers, and flaxdressers. Around 100 pupils attended the school at that time. By the time of the 1845 *Statistical Account* Kenmore itself had about 80 inhabitants. It was regarded as a very healthy area to live and it was noted that there were then six females between 74 and 94, with an average age of 85. In the parish as a whole one third of the total population of over 3,000 was aged under fifteen years. Gaelic was almost universally spoken but English was coming into greater use and understanding.

The hotel is acknowledged to be Scotland's oldest inn, established in 1572 when Sir Colin Campbell granted a lease of the land of Cobble Croft to his servant Hew Hay and his wife Christian Stanes, for an 'honest hostelrie' which should have sufficient bread and ale in readiness at all times to serve the people of the district. This 'hostellarie' was to be 'loftit' and have chimneys, doors and windows. Robert Burns visited the hotel in 1789. He was so impressed with the area and its picturesque village that he composed a romantic poem about it, which he wrote in pencil on the chimney breast in the bar. Now protected within a glass cover, it remains there to this day. The presence of the war memorial outside the church and the style of the men's clothes suggest that this photograph was taken around 1920. The hotel was then still named 'Breadalbane' but this was soon changed to the 'Kenmore' to avoid confusion with similarly named hotels in the area. The parish church was built in cruciform shape by William Baker in 1760 and incorporated the remains of a 1669 kirk. It was remodelled again in 1869 and the pinnacled tower was heightened to improve the visual effect. The pinnacles later became unsafe and were removed some years ago by the then minister, Kenneth MacVicar, who was concerned that his congregation might suddenly be reduced in numbers! The clock was installed around 1780 and is the second oldest in Perthshire.

The orphanage at Kenmore took in orphaned children from all over the Breadalbane estates, even from their English estates. At the time of the 1891 census there were eight children aged between five and sixteen years of age in residence. They were in the care of the Matron, Miss Maggie McLean, who was recorded as being 42 years of age, born in Kenmore and who spoke both Gaelic and English. In 1912 the orphanage was used to house some of the children orphaned by the sinking of the S.S. *Titanic*. The building was closed as an orphanage many years ago and is now a private house. Holder Hall, on the left, was built by Sir John Holder to serve as the village hall but was closed and demolished when a new school, which included a community centre, was opened in 1967.

Opposite: The original building on this site, about a mile east of Kenmore, was Balloch Castle which was built in 1550 for Sir Colin (Grey) Campbell of Glenorchy and was the cause of Inchadney village being moved up the river to be rebuilt as the present Kenmore village. In 1799 the fourth Earl of Breadalbane demolished the castle of Balloch and began building the present Taymouth Castle. Habitable by 1807, it was greatly extended in time for Lord Breadalbane's entertainment of Queen Victoria and the Prince Consort in September 1842. No expense was spared on the castle and its public rooms are outstanding examples of the opulence and refinements created by the best architects and craftsmen of the early nineteenth century. The central building has a cloistered colonnade and corner towers, whilst within the central tower a staircase was created that soars over 100 feet through all four storeys of the tower. Mounting expenses and death duties led to the Breadalbane Estates being broken up in 1922. The Taymouth estate was purchased by a business syndicate who, prior to the Second World War, operated the castle as a luxury hotel and turned the deer park into a golf course. During the Second World War the castle was requisitioned by the government and used as a hospital and convalescent home for Polish forces in Britain from 1940 to 1947. After the war it became the headquarters for Civil Defence Training in Scotland and for a short time it was used as a school for the children of American servicemen. In 1940 the ninth Earl had moved to Kinnell House at Killin. By 1946 all that was left of the once-vast estates was Kinnell House and a farm at Killin. Even the family mausoleum at Finlarig had crumbled into ruin. In 1948 he sold Kinnell House to Archibald Corrie MacNab, 22nd chief of MacNab, who thus re-purchased his family's ancestral home and lands which the first Marquis of Breadalbane had bought from the seventeenth MacNab chief in 1828. Today the golf course is one of the most popular in Scotland but the castle stands empty and forlorn. It is owned by the Mactaggart family and plans are currently afoot to reopen it as a hotel.

This model dairy was built around 1838 on a wooded knoll at the side of the main drive to Taymouth Castle. The dairy stands on the site of a tower which belonged to the chieftain of the MacGregor clan. The MacGregors had been expelled from the area in 1552 by Sir Colin Campbell of Glenorchy who had obtained a grant of these lands from the Crown by somewhat devious means. The building is a fantastic combination of sparkling local white quartz stone and rustic wood-columned porticos with a central belvedere and a bowed wing. Internally, it has marble floors and Dutch-tiled walls. On her visit to the castle in 1842 Queen Victoria visited the dairy and tried her hand at making butter with a silver-handled churn. It is many years since the building last functioned as a dairy. Long ago it was converted into a private dwelling, but has stood empty since 2001.

The gothic West Gate to Taymouth Castle was built around 1838 at the east end of the village square facing the parish church. The gateway, the Square, the main blocks of buildings and the church are arranged symmetrically in the English village style with the main road leading off north-west to the Kenmore Bridge. The building on the left was built as the Breadalbane Institute and has always been known locally as the 'Reading Rooms'. In former days it was used as a library and educational centre but after the break-up of the Breadalbane Estates in 1922 it served for many years as a trading store. Plans in the late 1930s to re-establish it as a library were thwarted by the outbreak of the Second World War and any prospects in post-war years were killed off by the introduction of a mobile library service to the village. When the Duke of Montrose attacked Tayside in 1644 he had set up his headquarters under a pear tree in a nearby orchard on the shores of Loch Tay. The tree was subsequently made into a massive table which was in the Graham family's possession for over 200 years. In 1884 Alma, Countess of Breadalbane, who was herself a descendant of Montrose presented the table to the Reading Rooms 'as a token of the peace and love which now unites Graham and Campbell, so long divided by war and hatred'. Nowadays the building is used as a playgroup centre and is hired out for small-scale functions. Its celebrated table has been removed to Taymouth Castle for its own protection. The photograph dates from the 1930s. The scene is basically unchanged, but nowadays the gate has been shorn of its creeper and sheep no longer mingle with motor traffic.

Around 1700 the village of Lawers on the north side of Loch Tay was an important terminal for the ferry from Ardtalnaig, which lies opposite on the south shore of Loch Tay where the main road came over the hills from the Sma' Glen and Crieff. The ruins of the houses down by the old harbour can still be seen in the woods at the foot of Lawers Burn and the old graveyard can be seen inside a walled enclosure in the middle distance beyond the burn. This photograph shows the ferryman's cottage and byre around the turn of the twentieth century. The cottage stood near the mouth of the burn, some distance from the landing stage, which was approached down a very steep track from the main road half a mile away on the hillside. Its occupant at the time of the 1891 census was Alexander Campbell with his wife and two teenage daughters. The landing stage was also a calling point for pleasure steamers plying between Killin and Kenmore. No boats call at Lawers nowadays and only the ruins remain of the ferry cottage and its outbuildings, but the old stone slipways and the rotting stumps of the timber landing stage can still be seen jutting out into the waters of the loch.

The Kirk of the Lady of Lawers was built in 1669 and was located near to the ferry crossing: it once had galleries on each arm of its T-Plan design. No-one knows for certain who the 'Lady of Lawers' really was, but she is thought to have been a Stewart of Appin, Argyll, who married a younger brother of the sixth Laird of Lawers. Famous as a remarkable seer, she made many prophecies, too many to be described here but most of which were fulfilled. For instance, in 1680 she forecast that the lands of MacNab would be joined to those of Breadalbane when two trees joined together on the isle of Inch Buie and grew as one. By a freak of nature, two trees on the island did grow together and the prophecy appeared to come true around 1828 when the Marquis of Breadalbane bought the bankrupt MacNab estate. Around the same time she prophesied the end of the Breadalbane family, forecasting that no line of the family would last for more than two generations and that 'in time the estates of Balloch will yield only one rent, then none at all, and the last laird will pass over Glenogle with a grey pony leaving nothing behind'. This prophecy was fulfilled in 1948 when the then earl sold his last property and he, together with his horse and groom, travelled south by train from Killin. The first church fell into disrepair at the beginning of the nineteenth century and a new mission church and manse were built close to the public road, the foundation stone being laid in 1833. The building is now in an even more ruinous state than shown in this photograph. Only its south and west gables are still standing, together with the lower windows of the middle section. The doorway has vanished but its aperture can still be seen. The Lady of Lawers is buried close beside her church.

Many years ago Lawers was a thriving village boasting a mission church (built in 1833 by the Marquis of Breadalbane at a cost of £685), a school, and both a lint mill and a meal mill. The Free Church had been established by the Society for Propagating Christian Knowledge in 1790 with funds from the late Lady Glenorchay's estate. She was a very pious lady and left a large sum of money to establish similar churches in the district. King James III of Scotland had granted the lands of Lawers to Sir Colin Campbell in 1473, in gratitude for Sir Colin's efforts in catching the murderers of his grandfather, James I. Sir Colin built a home on his lands, probably down by the loch side west of Lawers Burn, but this was destroyed during the Marquis of Montrose's raid on the district in 1645. The family then moved south to Strathearn where they purchased the Fordie estate near Comrie which they renamed 'Lawers' in memory of their former home. This view of the village looking west shows the road along the north side of Loch Tay which had been built as a toll road by the third Earl of Breadalbane at his own expense. It was the building of this road higher along the hillside that signalled the death knell of the original village huddled far below by the loch side around the mouth of Lawers Burn. The nearest building in the photograph is the old Toll Cottage, now the premises of 'Hand Carved Horn Services'. Its outward appearance is very little altered today. A modern house has been built immediately beyond it, but only the ruins remain of the further building in the photograph, which was the smithy. What appears to be a low wall beyond the tollhouse is actually the parapet of the bridge over the Lawers Burn opposite the old meal and sawmill. On the hillside are the crofters cottages of Cuiltrannich, now also in ruins.

This meal mill, which was also worked as a sawmill, was located on the far side of Lawers Burn. The mill buildings are in the left foreground and part of the smithy is visible across the road. Pigot's Directory of 1837 gives the miller's name as Duncan Graham. In 1888 it was Malcolm McLaren who doubled as both miller and the local tailor, but the 1891 census records Duncan Campbell as being the miller. The meal mill ceased working around 1927 and the sawmill around 1966; both had shared the same water wheel shown in the photograph. The water wheel has long since vanished and the building has been converted into the cottage that is now called 'The Old Mill'. Further down the burn, behind the photographer, is the first lint mill to be built by Hugh (Ewan) Cameron. He was born in Lawers in 1705 and, after training as a millwright, he travelled all over the Highlands constructing low-cost lint mills. It was he who taught the people of Breadalbane how to use spinning wheels and jack-reels. After a lifetime's work he retired to the Shian of Lawers and died there in 1817 at the age of 112 years.

At the time of the *New Statistical Account*, written in 1845, the Ben Lawers Hotel was the only public house in the seventeen miles between Killin and Kenmore. It was built as a temperance hotel at the side of the main road above the ferry pier and was originally known as the 'Croft House'. However, any thirsty travellers on the ferry had first to make a gruelling half-mile climb up a steep track before they could quench their thirst. The 'T' in the sign obviously stood for 'Temperance' and the hotel was not licensed for serving alcoholic drinks until around 1980. The sportily dressed car driver in the photograph stayed at the hotel for five days in August 1916 (he sent this photograph as a postcard). Apart from the porch having been extended along the length of the wall and the two blocked-off windows on the gable having been reinstated, the exterior of the hotel is unchanged. The lady standing by the porch next to what looks to be a deck chair leaning against the wall may be one of the staff or even the licensee, but the man in the white hat is more of a puzzle. He has a leather collecting-bag slung across his front, similar to what bus and tram conductors used to carry, and is wearing long boots but not a uniform. Could he have been the toll collector for the ferry?

Acharn lies on the south road from Kenmore to Killin, about two miles west of Kenmore. Its name means 'the field of the cairn'. The village was built at the end of the eighteenth century by the fourth Earl and first Marquis of Breadalbane in an effort to improve the condition of his Highland tenants. As well as housing, the Marquis provided each of his tenants with free grazing for two cows, work on the Taymouth estates, and he also built them a meal mill which was water-driven by the Acharn Burn. In Victorian times the village became a tourist attraction and artificial 'hermitages' were built to enhance the effect of the local waterfalls and impress the visitors. This view of the village shows the road leading southwards from the village centre towards the smithy and on to the spectacular Falls of Acharn. Around 1760 the third Earl of Breadalbane built an artificial hermitage here and even employed a professional guide for the benefit of visitors to the area. Sadly the hermitage is now a ruin. The large house on the right of the photograph is 'Pine Cottage'; its appearance is almost unchanged today, although it is now almost hidden behind tall hedges. The buildings beyond it have gone, as has the gabled house in the centre of the photo which has been replaced by a modern house. The row of cottages on the left have been modernised and the development is called 'Ballinlaggan'. A map of 1867 shows that the smithy was behind the row of cottages and there was a sawmill located behind Pine Cottage.

The gable end of Acharn's corn mill is on the left of the photograph, with worn stone steps leading up to a doorway above which a dovecote nestles between the eaves. The row of cottages with gardens fronting onto the road from Kenmore to Ardeonaig and Killin were part of the Marquis of Breadalbane's attempt in the 1790s to settle his tenants in a more industrious environment. In years gone by it was known locally as 'The Manufactory'. The scene is little changed today. The row of cottages shown in the photograph have a total of six eaves, but now have four eaves plus two skylights. Nowadays, there are two cottages in the centre plus one at each end. The large tree in the centre of the photograph has gone and has been replaced by the Parish Notice Board and a wooden bench seat, whilst the house in the far distance is now 'Tay Valley Lodges'. For a period in the 1970s the mill was converted into a craft centre, but nowadays it is a private house; however the line of steps up to the doorway (now a window) can still be discerned, although the roadway is now at a higher level.

Another view of the village centre at Acharn, looking west with the meal mill in the middle distance and the row of estate cottages on the right. The steps leading up to the gable door of the mill can be clearly seen. The road divided at this point. The left fork ran southwards through the upper part of the village past Pine Cottage and the smithy and became a track to the Falls of Acharn, whilst the main road forked to the right and crossed an old stone bridge on its way to Ardtalnaig, Ardeonaig and Killin. This postcard was sent in July 1911 and the writer talks about going out for the day from Aberfeldy on a charabanc and returning on a motor coach. Such modern excitement!

Another photograph from Acharn, dating from around 1912, of estate cottages with log-columned porches. These appear to be very spacious homes indeed with several rooms and lots of large windows. They were built around 1860 and stand on the main road through the village, west of the bridge across the Acharn Burn and opposite the former post office which is built in the identical style. The cottages still look in almost exactly the same condition as shown here.

Like the cottages shown on the previous page, which stand on the opposite side of the road, the exterior of the former post office is virtually unchanged from almost a century ago. In the photo, the sign on the building says 'A. McArthur – Grocer and Clothier'. He was a merchant and is listed in Leslie's Directory of 1889/90 as 'Archibald McArthur, grocer and tailor'. He was succeeded by his widow Catherine sometime around 1910 and the business first appears as a post office in the Valuation Rolls of 1911–12. It remained a family business for many years; Leslie's Directory of 1935/36 lists the occupiers as being John McArthur, sub-postmaster and grocer, and Duncan McArthur, tailor. In common with many rural post offices, the facility has been withdrawn in recent years and the building is now Haugh Cottage, offering bed & breakfast accommodation. The photograph shows a well-to-do man – possibly the local landowner? – standing behind his private carriage in which his groom sits waiting for him, whilst the postmaster and proprietor stands outside the post office. Note the rain-soaked road – a journey in a carriage along the south road in bad weather must have been a very muddy experience!

The village of Ardeonaig is situated at the mouth of the Finglen Burn where it enters Loch Tay and was once a ferry crossing point to Lawers on the opposite bank. It lies on the old main road from Killin to Kenmore, before the present main road on the north side of the loch was built by the Earl of Breadalbane in the eighteenth century. The name means the heights of Saint Adamnan who was associated with the area. He was the ninth Abbot of Iona, biographer of St Columba and died in AD 704. Ardeonaig was the starting point for the famous overland raid in 1612 by the twelve sons of the MacNab chieftain on the Clan Neish stronghold on Loch Earn to avenge the theft of their Christmas provisions by the Neish family. They carried a boat over the hills to Loch Earn from where they rowed out to Neish Island and took its defenders by surprise. They slew all the Neish clansmen except for one small boy and returned home with the severed head of the chieftain as a present for their father. This photograph was taken at harvest time around 1910, looking from the hillside northwards over the village with Loch Tay in the background. All the stone-built buildings still survive. The large building in the centre (marked with a cross) is the Ardeonaig Hotel, an ancient hostelry which is known to have been selling ale to drovers as early as 1649. Its earlier name was Tigh-na-Linne (the house of the pool) and in the seventeenth century ale was brewed on Thursdays to be tasted by Cunstaris (inspectors) on Sundays. By law the hotel was forbidden to sell ale on Sundays before preaching was over! The large building on the left is the old schoolhouse which closed in 1986 with only four pupils on the roll, down from a peak of around 50. It is nowadays a private house.

An early Edwardian view of the hamlet of Craggan, a little way down the road from Ardeonaig towards Killin. Loch Tay lies unseen at the foot of the mountains on the right, the largest mountain being Ben Lawers itself. In the foreground two local worthies pass the time of day in the sunshine, whilst in the distance a man holds a little child's hand as they pass Ballinloan, probably returning from the post office which stands on the right of the bend in the road. The house on the left-hand side of the photograph and the two nearest ones on the right have long since gone (only a few stones mark where they once stood), but the former post office still stands although it is now a private house. Beyond it the road passes Croftnabeallie and its kennels and Croftshennach on its way to Killin.

Cattle drink their fill from Ardeonaig Burn in this winter view of the old mill at Ardeonaig. Looking eastwards towards Kenmore, it was situated on the right-hand side of the road immediately after the bridge by the Ardeonaig Hotel. Even in this early photograph there does not appear to be any activity going on at the mill and its buildings look to be in poor condition. It was demolished many years ago and there is practically nothing left, although a keen eye can still discern the outline of walls and a few stones which obviously once formed part of this eighteenth century centre of local industry.

Croftnabeallie stands in the foreground, the post office nestles by the roadside to its right and Loch Tay lies concealed beyond them in this 1904 photograph of Ben Lawers seen from Ardeonaig. The mountain is owned nowadays by the National Trust for Scotland, which has built a visitor centre at its foot, and is the richest source of alpine flowers in the British Isles; the *Saxifraga cernia* (the drooping saxifrage) is found nowhere else in Britain. The hillside is dotted with abandoned shielings, all that remain of an ancient agricultural custom in which the farming folk and their cattle, after the long hard winter, moved for three or four months to the fresher summer pastures higher up. Shielings were built from stones lying around and were roofed with branches and sods. Here the cattle would recover their strength after the hard winter and fatten up in readiness for sale at the autumn trysts. Meanwhile the women and children would spin and make butter and cheese, some of which they used themselves and the remainder they sold on their next visit to a local fair.

The driver of a two-horse carriage waits patiently for custom outside the Tighanloan Hotel at Fearnan, some four miles west of Kenmore where the road from Glen Lyon and Fortingall joins the main road running along the north side of Loch Tay. The left-hand portion of the building served as Fearnan Post Office. A sign bearing the name 'Stewart' appears over the doorway and the man standing under it is probably John Stewart himself who was licensee of the hotel for many years. The village of 'Stronfernan' was created by the Earl of Breadalbane around the same time as Kenmore. It comprised about 24 families and by 1836 its population was as high as 150. The Robertsons of Clan Donnachie was the principal family of the area. Behind the hotel was the meal mill worked by the humble John MacGregor who, in the early 1800s, managed to send his five surviving sons to be educated at Edinburgh University. All five graduated with degrees and three of them became ministers of the church. As well as the hotel, which was originally a temperance hotel, the village had its own school but this was closed in 1967 when the new school was opened in Kenmore. The building was extensively remodelled in 1938 when an entirely new frontage was built onto the three right-hand bays which comprised the hotel, considerably increasing its size. The former post office section of two bays remained the same but nowadays form part of the hotel and have been fronted by a small lounge bar.

A man and a boy out fishing on Loch Tay rest their oars while they watch the *Queen of the Loch* slowly approaching Fearnan Pier from the Kenmore direction. This would have been her first call on the way to Killin at the other end of the loch. The wooden pier was located a few yards down the road from Tighanloan Hotel. Nothing remains nowadays except for the stone slipway which jutted out into the water alongside it.

Ardtalnaig village is situated on the south side of Loch Tay, six miles south west of Kenmore. Its name means 'the high pass' and it guarded a main drove route to Crieff and Comrie. The old road still exists as a track which skirts Ben Chonzie and reaches Crieff via Glen Almond and the A822 road down the Sma' Glen or Comrie via Glen Lednock. Many years ago there also used to be a ferry service across the loch to Lawers. The early kings of Scotland had a hunting lodge here, the Castle of Tay, which stood on the present site of Milton Farm. The area abounded in wild life and it is said that there were many wolves in the area even as late as the seventeenth century. This photograph, looking east, shows the village post office around 1930; the house beyond with the car parked outside offered accommodation to visitors. Beyond the car, the road dips and bends to the right to cross the Ardtalnaig Burn by a narrow stone bridge. Immediately beyond the bridge is an area to the left known as Miltown which was the site of an old lint mill built by the celebrated Hugh Cameron of Lawers. The post office and its adjoining cottage (now private houses) have survived but the darker building beyond them is no longer there. Gone, too, are the old smithy and the school.

The Society for Propagating Christian Knowledge (SPCK) began operating in Scotland in 1701 and founded many schools in remote areas. In 1716 it noted that there were 400 persons in the Glen Lochay area without a school and decided that one should be established at Innischaorach, the schoolmaster to be paid a salary of £15 per year. A stone-built school was duly constructed on the north side of the road at a distance of five miles up the glen from Bridge of Lochay and just before the Allt Lebhain burn. It was maintained from the income of a sum of 6,000 merks Scots, bequeathed in 1740 by the Rev. Archibald Campbell, minister of Weem, for the purpose of maintaining schools in detached portions of that parish. (A merk had a value of 13/4d or 67p in modern-day money). In those days village schoolmasters taught the reading of English and Gaelic, writing and arithmetic. Schoolmistresses taught sewing and knitting of stockings. Latin and Greek were only taught in the larger schools such as Killin and Kenmore. By the time this photograph was taken in 1929 the number of pupils was down to 10, all taught by a Miss Smith, but the school survived for several more years in spite of being in an isolated location. It has since been converted into a private house and extended slightly but is still instantly recognisable as the old school building.

Glen Lochay was once the hunting area of Stewart kings and royal charters say it was 'very rich in deir', but this party obviously had no intention of hunting or doing any serious walking. The scarcity of leaves on the trees and the party's heavy top coats indicates that the time is late autumn or winter whilst their footwear suggests they have recently alighted from a motor car. Indeed the gentleman, with his magnificent Edwardian moustache and winged collar and tie, is dressed more suitably for a walk down Princes Street than on a rough track in the wilds of Perthshire in 1929. The road up Glen Lochay towards Batavaim eventually petered out into a rough track. Had they literally come to the end of the road?

Although the area bordering Loch Tay and its principal tributaries, the Lochay and the Dochart, has always been suitable for sheep farming, agriculture has always been a precarious living. The first *Statistical Account of Scotland*, written in 1795, gives the wages of agricultural labourers as being 1/- (5p) per day unless they provided their own food, in which case their daily wage could rise to between 1/3d and 1/11d (6.25p to 9.4p) per day. Even 50 years later, when the *New Statistical Account* was compiled in 1845, their wages were still only 1/3d per day in winter and up to 2/4d (11.8p) per day in the summer. These rates were said to be 'quite high'. Indoor servants received even less. The wages of male indoor servants rose from £7–£10 per year in 1795 to £10–£14 per year in 1845 whilst the corresponding wages of female domestic servants were £2–£3 per year in 1795 and £4–£6 per year in 1845. The ploughman's rate of pay had increased considerably by the time this photograph was taken in the late 1920s, but the method of ploughing would have been familiar to his Victorian ancestors. Even in 1845 it was commented that agriculture needed capital investment if it was to significantly improve and that a fair amount of cultivated land would be better off reverting to pasture. A recent visit to the location of the photograph, on the banks of the River Lochay with Boreland House in the background, shows that this is exactly what has happened here: the ground that is being so laboriously ploughed by the man and his two horses is once again pasture land.

Rob Roy MacGregor was born in 1671 at Glengyle at the head of Loch Katrine but later moved to Portnellan in Glen Dochart where he speculated in the cattle trade. Unfortunately his speculations turned out to be financially disastrous for him and in 1712 the Duke of Montrose seized his estates further south as security for unpaid debts. It was then that Rob Roy moved a few miles along Glen Dochart to this house at Corriechaorach from where he ran a profitable 'protection racket' at his neighbours' expense, promising to safeguard their herds against cattle thieves. In 1715, along with the rest of his clan, he was outlawed for his part in the abortive Jacobite rebellion against the Crown. He then turned his attention to raiding the territories of his arch-enemy the Duke of Montrose and other members of the Graham clan. Eventually he gained a royal pardon and moved south to the Braes of Balquhidder. He became a respectable citizen and died in his bed on 28 December 1734. He is buried in the churchyard at Balquhidder. Very little remains of his house at Corriechaorach which is on the hillside on the left-hand side of the A85 road heading west towards Crianlarich, a little way beyond Luib. The photograph was taken in the early years of the twentieth century and nowadays only the right-hand (west) gable is still standing.